A Magic Presence

Also by Ruth Dorrien Pennyman: *The Intruder*, Avalon Editions York (1982) ISBN 0-904833-17-8

Also by Ilse Cornwall-Ross

Franz Klemmer, An Artist in the War 1914-1918, Ursula Brodhage, Nuernberg, 1995 ISBN 3-9802979-3-4

A Season of Mellow Fruitfulness, John Keats in Winchester, 1819, Ilex Terrace Press, 1995 ISBN 0-9526333-0-2.

Chapter 7 Ruth the poet, Ruth the Friend in *The Last Pennymans of Ormesby Volume II 1945 – 1983,* Bargate Publications, Richmond, North Yorkshire (2009) ISBN 978-0-9545789-4-7

A Magic Presence

An anthology of Poems
by
Ruth Pennyman (1893 – 1983)

Selected, edited and with an introduction by
Ilse Cornwall-Ross
with illustrations by Joan Mullins

First Edition 2011
Bargate Publications
40, Bargate,
Richmond,
North Yorkshire,
DL10 4QY
www.bargatepublications.co.uk (01748) 821534

© Ilse Cornwall-Ross & W.G. Hugonin 2011

All rights reserved. No part of this book may be reproduced, stored or introduced into a retrieval system or transmitted in any form or by any means (electronic, mechanical, photocopying, recording or otherwise) without the prior permission of the publisher.

ISBN 978-0-9545789-5-4

Overall book design concept: Ilse Cornwall-Ross
Photographs for cover: Liz Hayward
Cover Graphics: Bargate Photographic

The Editor

Ilse Cornwall-Ross is a graduate and postgraduate (as a mature student) of Teesside University (then Poly), where she was subsequently employed as a research assistant for three years.

After moving to Winchester/Hampshire following this, she worked as a lecturer and teacher. During that time she researched and published her book on John Keats in Winchester.
Now semi-retired, she is undertaking research on the life of Yorkshire born Elizabeth Montagu (1718-1800), who later became the first 'bluestocking' and is buried in Winchester Cathedral.

Ilse has recently renewed her contact with Ormesby Hall and has helped to run poetry workshops there.

Introduction

Ruth Pennyman was well known for her public role as a patron of the arts in the North East of England. She produced Shakespearean plays, provided a base for Joan Littlewood's Theatre Workshops at Ormesby Hall and she worked with Michael Tippett on the libretto for *Robin Hood*, his first opera. Ruth helped establish *Opera Nova* and fostered a tradition of community theatre in the area, writing plays, attracting renowned artists and composers to Ormesby Hall and lending Teesside Youth Theatre a much-valued rehearsal space.

However, her very private work as a poet is less known. Yet - writing poetry was an important part of her creative life and served her as a retreat from her work at Ormesby Hall, first as the wife of a country squire and then, for some 22 years, as a widow in charge of the day-to-day running of a stately home.

Ruth had the extraordinary gift of making everyone with whom she came into contact special. She engaged with a large variety of people – young and old, of different backgrounds – with scant regard for convention or social hierarchy. She was immensely sociable and she supported and encouraged creative endeavours of all kinds. Her frequent trips to London kept her in touch with the art world there, too.

Hidden beneath the public persona there was the private person we can discern in her poems. They convey her love of life and her power of observation. She was not concerned with form and had no theoretical training in writing. However, her intimate knowledge of Greek drama and mythology and of Shakespearean language and thought is very noticeable in her poetry.

Ruth said of herself: ' I seem to have written, drawn and played with colour all the life I can remember [1]). Her creative background is well documented by her younger sister Katherine in a script written in 1954, entitled *50 Years Ago*. This provides a vivid insight into Ruth's formative childhood experiences, then aged around 11 years. At that time her father was the vicar of Dogmersfield near Winchfield in Hampshire and life in the Rectory, though financially restricted, sounds blissful. At this early age Ruth and her sister helped to 'roll off programme after programme for village concerts.' We read about the importance of their mother's bureau in the drawing-room: 'always the hub of any sitting-room of hers', about the piano where her mother 'used to play accompaniments to regional songs' and the blackboard which was 'usually covered with Ruth's drawings, nearly always horses in those days.'

Reminiscences about games are precursors of sentiments expressed in some of Ruth's poems. 'What exciting games you invented for me with my dolls and toy monkeys under the rhododendrons and on the lawn' Katherine writes and 'the fallen petals of the great crimson-mauve flowers you turned into plates and cups and saucers, the daisies on the lawn were picked for ice-cakes, leaves for bread and butter and all was grist to your magic mill of 'let's pretend''. Katherine refers to the afternoon when they returned from their first journey abroad – to Rapallo- when Ruth, aged around 11 years, 'wrote and staged an Italian play on the lawn'. 'Dressed up with bright scarves round our heads, we acted our play of two little girls, one who wanted to leave home – you (Ruth) of course – and one who didn't'.

Obviously the two little girls had plenty of opportunities for developing their creativity. Katherine recalls Nanny Godfrey who 'came to the rescue over so many important and vital things' and she reminds Ruth of being 'sung to for the first five minutes in bed, before the night nurse took charge:

Suppose the little cowslip
Should close its tiny cup,
And say 'I'm such a humble flower,
I'd better not grow up.'

Then she retracts this remark by saying: 'Though I'm not sure Nanny sang to you, for you were the brave kind who took night as well as day, in your stride.' [2])

These childhood experiences were vital foundations for Ruth's later life – as an art student, as a nurse in WW1, as an actress, a producer of plays and a poet.

It was my very good fortune to be befriended by Ruth, after we had first met at a party and had discovered many common interests. This friendship led to an invitation by Ruth for us to come and live in an apartment at Ormesby Hall, in the mid 1970s, when our newly built house had to be modified. During this time (and whilst I was doing a degree course in Literature at the then Teesside Poly) I encouraged and helped Ruth to edit some of her existing poems and also inspired her to write new poetry.

In preparing the poems for publication, I have edited them very lightly and not changed their form so as to retain the spirit of her work and the way she intended to have it read. In this collection I have brought together almost Ruth's entire output – poems previously published in THE INTRUDER, poems typed up, duplicated and circulated in VERSE, RHYME AND DOGGEREL, poems unearthed in uncatalogued material in the archive at Ormesby Hall and some found in Christmas cards that she had written.

Regrettably, I have not been able to date the poems. However, I have presented them loosely organized in themes, starting and finishing with poetry 'around Ormesby Hall'. For two poems, DEAD and SONG FOR SARAH, background information is given in the references on page 112, as I witnessed the process of the event/s that prompted Ruth to write the poems and her reaction to them.

It is my hope that this collection of poems will bring to life Ruth's multi-faceted and powerfully creative being to the people who loved her and remember her. Moreover, as a testament of her times and her special position in Ormesby Hall, her poems enable us to share the mind of this extraordinary, courageous woman, who led a life which was at once conventional and yet very unconventional for her times. Her beautiful home, Ormesby Hall and its grounds, gave her the background and ambience for writing. Maybe visitors will also find inspiration here and sense her 'Magic Presence', as I did.

Ilse Cornwall-Ross
April 2011

1.   Introduction to *The Intruder*, Ruth Dorrien Pennyman, Avalon Editions, York 1982
2.   *50 Years Ago*, Katherine Connolly, neé Knight, 1954 Hampshire County Record Office 37A08

Acknowledgements:-

I would like to thank the following people:-

Bill Hugonin for allowing me to make use of Ruth's poems; Liz Hayward, Ormesby Hall NT, for her generous general assistance, granting me access to the Ormesby Hall Archive and for supplying photographs for the book cover; Joan Mullins for her beautiful illustrations based on photographs and my family for their interest and help. Last but not least I am indebted to Mark Whyman who rekindled my interest in Ruth Pennyman when he invited me to contribute a chapter to *The Last Pennymans of Ormesby Volume II*. In addition to publishing this book, he took photographs around Ormesby Hall, as directed by me, which served as a stimulus for the illustrations. His enthusiastic and indefatigable support - from one Ruth admirer to another - was invaluable.

It is with great delight that the National Trust and all associated with Ormesby Hall welcome this new anthology of poems written by a remarkable lady, Ruth Pennyman, who was the last of the Pennyman family to live here. She is still remembered in the local community as a creative, artistic and influential woman of strong socialist views, who brought kindness and joy into the lives of many people in the community on her doorstep, as well as many further afield.

She loved her historic rural home and filled it with creative endeavours and interesting people, many connected with the Arts nationally, yet she still found time to write poetry of great sensitivity, insight and depth. Some of these poems appeared in the 'The Intruder', published in 1982, others are so far unpublished, but all reflect the inspiration which she gained from living in such a peaceful oasis of beauty on the southern edge of the Tees Valley.

The editor, Ilse Cornwall-Ross, not only gives us access to the poems, but we get to know Ruth better through someone who knew her well personally, and who spent many hours with her in her widowhood, discussing literature and composing poetry in this very special environment.

More can be learned about this extraordinary lady, Ruth Pennyman and her husband Colonel Jim, through reading the fascinating detailed biographical works by Mark Whyman, *The Last Pennymans of Ormesby, volumes 1 & 2*, and also through visiting their lovely historic home in Teesside.

Ormesby Hall is now in the hands of the National Trust, whose remit, set out by Jim in his 'Memorandum of Wishes', includes the task of keeping alive the name of the Pennyman family and perpetuating links with the performing arts as much as possible, and this precious volume is well placed to do just that.

The poetic tradition continues in work carried out with local community groups and young people who have been introduced to Ruth's artistry on site and who have in turn written their own poetic responses to her life story, her poetry and her home. Ruth would have delighted in these voyages of self discovery which owe their existence to her untutored, and she would claim, uneducated, talent for responding to people and places in poetry.

I would like to thank Ilse personally for all her diligence in producing an anthology to reflect with love and respect Ruth Pennyman, this amazing creative personality.

Liz Hayward, the National Trust, Ormesby Hall

Ormesby Hall - West front
Mark Whyman

CONTENTS

Dream	1
Courtship (previously Rendez-Vous)	2
Song for Sarah	5
Light	7
Creative Creatures (later renamed Intruder 1)	9
A Fish Muses	12
Biologist	15
Walk	19
The Ginger Tom	21
Child on a Sunny Morning	25
Jingle for Sputnik	28
Search	31
Far	33
Home – Stray Kitten	35
Dead	36
Power Crisis	37
Excerpts from Aphrodite (ii)	41
Excerpts from Aphrodite (iii)	43
Punic Coin	46
Ankor Wat	48
Africa	50
Drumbeat	53
Mosque	54
News (Vietnam)	56
Beware	58
Superior People	60
Geriatric Ward – An old man	62
Geriatric Ward – An old woman	66
Country Wedding	69
Spring Salute	72

Compassion	73
Sunday Morning	75
Teresa's Song	76
Coombe	77
Whitsun	79
June	81
Christmas	84
Christmas Dialogue	85
Songs for Magnificat Open the Door	88
Herod Augustus	91
First Footing	92
Doggerel for Winter	95
November 24th	97
Nightmare	99
Lament	102
Widow	104
The Intruder (2)	106
House	109
Goodwill towards Men	111

Dream

I woke from dreaming
full of the peace which passeth understanding,
a diver coming up
from the depths undredged.

I was in a room, quietly mending something.
I was in a room
with somebody I loved and who loved me.

The strangest thing about this strangest dream
was that I do not know
whose was the magic presence.
I do not know – I think I did not know.

We were not speaking.
We were not making love.
This was the calm deeper than any passion,
the final journey's end.

All through the following day
I floated angelical;
earth agonies – earth noises–
came muted and transmuted
like far off barking dogs
through the Elysian air.

Plato smiled in his heaven
because his wandering halves
at last had found each other
and were at rest.

Courtship (originally Rendez-Vous)

Where?

Here.

I can't see.

No one can.
One can only feel around in the dark.
Men and women have to – learn to.

It's lonely.

It is rather.

Is that your hand?

Yes.

It's not very warm.

No.
If you held it – it might be.

How do I know who you are?

How do I?
We have to guess –
if you moved a little nearer we might kiss.

But I don't know what you look like.

Of course not.
It's too dark. We have to guess.
Be careful how you move.

Where do you come from?

I don't know.

Where are you going?

I often wonder.

Don't go.
Your hand is a little warmer.

So is yours.

Why do you think?

Perhaps because they are holding each other.

Perhaps.
Don't let go.

Why?

I'm afraid in the dark.

So am I.

Then don't leave me.
Your hand is large, are you a tall man?

Yours is small, are you a girl?

Yes – No.

Your hand is warm. Will you go on holding mine?

Perhaps.

Song for Sarah[1]

I caught a leopard in a net of gold.
Sideways he looked at me and licked my hands.
We do not speak our thoughts.
Instead we sing together,
Michael and all angels play the tune.
Through the gold meshes we perceive the world
hurtling down supermarkets,
chasing its food and status,
famished for what we live on.
Through the gold meshes we throw it crumbs -
manna from starry spaces overhead.

I hold a leopard in a net of gold.
Will gold nets hold fast nor ever sag?
Nor let us drop into the supermart,
that nightmare place where angels furl their wings,
where Michael bleeds under the dragon's teeth.
(Oh no – don't look – it's dizzy looking down.)
While gods sit rock-like in the deep blue sky
we'll swing in safety, laughing at the sun.
The golden net will hold its treasury.

Light

First the silver rim.
The window etched against
the dark within.
Then growing in the irresistible tide
the inundation pouring from the sun,
the radient liquid soon to flood the earth,
a corner of the dressing table gleams.
A mirror echoing back reflected light.
As our planet earth
rotates its way through black infinity
and turns towards the sun
my room swims into view;
ghost pale and immaterial
like some astral emanation.
Then flooding inwards
an angle of my fourpost bed appears
and I am caught up in the miracle.
Light seeps into my brain,
light drowns my heart.
I am lifted up,
a wisp of seaweed in the racing tide.
Then I believe all things are possible -
dreams will dissolve into reality.
As the earth makes from darkness into light,
we shall become all that we long to be.
All life will grow together,
the barriers will fall down
like Jericho walls – when the seven times trumpets
sound.
As the birds sing to the dawn, we shall sing

like a great choir, we shall sing all together.
We shall see Heaven on Earth and Earth in Heaven.
We shall fall down before the Royal Throne where love reigns – after the long agony – at last triumphant.

Creative Creatures (later renamed 'The Intruder 1')

Stop talking. I don't want the newspapers.
Turn off the radio and television –
daemonic voices breathing out of depths
unknown, steeped in the mysteries,
are speaking; I can hear no other sound.
The Priestess reels intoxicated on.
The God is speaking through her from the deep
uncharted regions beneath consciousness.
In black infinity
I float above the world
as I stare, weightless, at the earthy rim.
Imagined stars swell into galaxies,
time ceases, outward things fade into dreams
and dreams take over solid substances.

I have to seem still living in this place
but I'm not here; I have departed thence.
I won't pay bills nor will I answer letters.
The bell rings, let it ring.
We're out of bread!
The people down the road
are coming in for drinks. The library books
are overdue. My hair is lank
and looks like seaweed, but
I AM ALIVE.

Perhaps I came like seaweed
out of the depths –

a minor Aphrodite;
for I am deep in love
and memories of other worlds
cling all about me.
I move clumsily in this one –
yet I am more alive than any mortal.

I AM A GOD. I SEE – I FEEL – I KNOW.
The miracle has happened once again,
the terrible excitement has returned,
the cup is filling up
with the intoxicating secret brew.
I am possessed and Dionysos reels
through the drab world – setting it all aflame.

The telephone – the telephone is ringing.
Damn it and blast it – may it rot in Hell.
'Hullo. Oh yes. I'd love to see you all
some time – some day- of course – I'll let you know.
I am not sure what are my future plans.'
I have no plans. Only this miracle
working within me. The voice driving on,
the tension which burns up the petty hours.
'I am expecting friends
and one has come already.'

I am with Dionysos, he is breathing
into my eyes and ears and singing heart.
'Yes, an old friend, quite unexpected, came –
of course, I'd love to bring the car and picnic.
I'll write – I'll telephone – I'll ring you back

tomorrow – next week – or the weekend after.
- Perhaps'.

A Fish Muses

And we are beautiful –
but he was blind.
His friends were fishermen,
they thought of us as fodder;
something to fill their pockets,
feed their children.

When we lay gasping out our lives,
struggling for breath,
he did not pity us.
He noticed sparrows
and lilies of the field
but
we shining creatures
moving like quicksilver,
till we are dragged ashore,
he let us die.

Once they say
He filled a net
up to the very brim.
We could have broken it.
He held us in
to please his friends.
Whole families were wiped out
they say
that day.
Whole tribes lay
gasping out their lives –
a silver pile,
tarnishing slowly

on the stony quay.

He is not even animal.
They say
he walks upon the water
so
He does not know
the agony of creatures
who live above
in air
and strangely,
very strangely,
reverse the natural state
and gasp for breath
when sinking under water,
as we do when they haul us
into air.

He cannot sink –
perhaps He cannot die
and so
he does not know
the long, long struggle
for survival,
for breath, for food,
for darting shining life.

For life, for life.
They say
we led the way –
our jellied ancestors
invented life.
They ate, they moved,

they felt both pain and pleasure,
they brought into the world
this miracle, this treasure.
I don't suppose
He knows.

Biologist

Who do you think you are?

I often wonder.

Giving yourself such airs.

Oh! Do I?

Sometimes you make me laugh.

Oh! Do you?

You make me laugh, you insect of an hour.
Perhaps I should not call you even that.
Insects in many ways are more developed;
organised with admirable efficiency.
You crawl about the earth – they run,
they dart, they fly, they dance on flowery stalks;
often they are the product
of metamorphosis.
You lurched clumsily – head foremost – into the world,
you accidental creature, like them
of random evolution.

I often feel like that, how well you put it.

Was it a good idea to stand on your hind legs?
You would be much more firmly set on four.
You could run faster, jump a longer distance.

If you possessed the steel and velvet muscles
of that stray cat you could leap off the earth
onto great Venus or alarming Mars
without the tangle of technology
you have assembled to entrap the world.
Who do you think you are?

I sometimes think – I sometimes even know –
I am a Man,
Immortal Son of God.
No random evolution made me that.
The strangest metamorphosis
is my future fate,
stranger than any insect's.

How then do you expect finally to emerge?

I cannot tell you.

But this is something that should be explored.
It has tremendous implications for the future
and value to a scientist – please continue.

I cannot.

Why? I have my notebook ready.

I do not know.

But this is totally absurd. You must know.
What are your grounds for this assumption?

I have none.

No proofs?

None.

You make me laugh.

Walk

Diogenes would like a walk
and so would I.
Up the long winding lane,
towards the farm
and down to meet the village.
The hedgerows are so high,
the lane so narrow,
one half is barred by shadow.
We will walk on the sunny side
and sniff for field mice
and count the wild flowers jostling each other,
struggling towards the sun –
bluebell and bracken,
wood anemone,
the purple vetch and speedwell's heavenly blue
and ragged robin and the small white star
which climbs and climbs – clinging to anything.
Blue borage in great clumps
and buttercups.
The winding path, a short cut to the village,
is overgrown by green exuberant June.
Great loops of bramble wind about my legs.
In autumn weighted down with blackberries,
wild parsley stands so high
that I could hide in it.
The nettles ramp,
ivy climbs everywhere –
the elegant pointed star,
beloved of the Greeks,
beloved of Dionysos,

mortal immortal – bringer of happiness –
who twined it in his tangled shining hair.

The Ginger Tom

I am that I am.
I am swifter than the wind.
My muscles are of steel,
steel and silk – nothing overtakes me.
I flash, I glide like a red streak,
always in hiding.
My teeth are like daggers,
my eyes shine in the night.
Coals of fire in the dark.
I have a ranker smell
than a fox.
My mother moaned and yelped pushing me out
in some decaying alley.
Unwillingly I came,
outcast of the world,
no part of any tribe,
no slave of human kind.
I hide. I steal. I kill.
I hate – often I lust;
for I am strong in summer.
In winter I go limping
and near starvation.
That tear has never mended
and half my ear is gone.
It wracks me in the frost.
When summer comes, I lust
and cannot find a female.
Sometimes I find one,
yet I cannot use her.
She has sold herself

to humans for their food
and they have taken, in exchange, her nature.
There is a special one
who wracks my blood and dreams.

I hate her, yet I cannot let her be.
I crouch at night
outside the place she lives in.
Once I got in.
There was food there.
A great bone, succulent with meat,
but dead – dead.
It had been dead for ages.
Men came
to corner – to catch me – to kill me.
In the open nothing can pass me
but enclosed within walls
I saw the world outside
through open spaces
and leapt to regain it.
Invisible barriers – terrible magic,
hard as iron, transparent as ice –
flung me back.
Panic gripped me.
This is the end – the dark,
the thing which all my life
I fly from. I fight.
This is something worse
than cold, hunger fear
to be fought – to be raced from.
If I must, I must face
even this.
I must fight the unkillable,

I must kill death,
bite with my dagger teeth,
tear with my scimitar claws.
Why? Why? Why?
Why do they hate me?
I am that I am.
But she is as they have made her.

She is fat and sleek.
When it freezes outside,
they call her in.
They give her food.
Never need she search for it,
run for it, kill for it.
A kind soft voice
which she answers
calls her in.
(What was that?
Some sound echoes through the ground
over there in the jungle.
My every nerve twitches.
Listen! Listen!)
Once I was crouching outside
and the voice called.
Something inside me melted.
Perhaps it was my heart.
A frozen lump turned to water.
I answered very softly,
but I knew the voice knew
and would not let me in –
knew I should stay outside for ever;
hunted and hated.
Yet, sometimes in dreams –

perhaps my mother's mother
or my mother's mother's mother
got inside those places and those hearts —
for sometimes in dreams
(What was that?
Something moved over there in the jungle.
Don't quiver, don't panic.
Freeze!)
Sometimes in dreams,
before they turn nightmare,
I sit by a fire
and wash myself
without fear, without hate,
my claws furled within
my velvet pads.
My panic heart at rest,
at rest.

Child On a Sunny Morning

Run. Tumble. Shout.
Blow up the trumpets in the golden air.
Unfurl the banners,
toss them to the skies.
The swifts lunge and swing
and shriek their happiness.
The air is shining,
shining all the grass;
the trees are singing out
and throw their velvet shadows
on the lawn.

Under the copper beech
Titania gleams,
laughing at Oberon
in golden spangled suit,
who blows her kisses.
Crispin comes bouncing out,
his eyes like polished marbles,
looking for something moving he can chase,
anything will do –
a leaf, a skimming swallow, a grey squirrel.
'Come on, good boy. I'll race you to the ha-ha'.
Tamarisk glides out into the sun
and rolls her shining fur upon the grass
and slinks into the blue and gold jungle
of the delphiniums.
Her green eyes gleam,
the pupils shrink into a thread of dark.
She whisks her tail

as so do I;
for both our hearts are shining
like this morning.

Let's run away,
let's take a picnic up into the woods.
Let's paddle in the river
and race barefooted on the pebbly sand.
Let's run away
into the blue hills with Titania
and Oberon and Tamarisk and Crispin.

Jingle for Sputnik

We have to die
you and I,
I know.
Do you?
It's true.
Everything, everything living
must go back to the earth;
vanishing, melting like snow.
Like a dream,
like a beam of light
suddenly snuffed
in the night.

Your amazing translucent eyes
which can see in the dark,
your pointed ears more sensitive than mine,
your velvet and steel body, apparently boneless,
your subtle brain intent on survival.
You never swallow a fishbone,
you never miscalculate
those miraculous leaps.
You are infinitely cautious,
ruthlessly determined
to live.
You have nine lives
but no tenth.

Do you guess the mess that will be you?
Do you know
it will be so?
The foe

we cannot vanquish
lies in wait
for you and me.
But we humans
have invented a safety device
to carry us over the sea
which will drown you.
You narrowly escaped
drowning at birth
on this earth.
All your brothers and sisters
were drowned blind.
How unkind –
never mind,
you survived for your beauty.
But beauty won't carry you farther.
Only goodness will do that
so say the wise.
But this is surmise.

Can you remember Egypt?
Where you were worshipped as a god?
There, divine royal blood
and elaborate burial
ensured survival.
Because you were buried in a pyramid palace,
wrapped in gold,
you could live forever.
How the poor slaves
bought and sold
like beasts in the market place
must have envied you,
as they heaved the stones

for your tremendous tomb.
They must have known that soon
they would die, exhausted,
and be buried like rats.
Forgotten.
   Forgotten.
      Forgotten.

But today
we all have a soul.
Immortality, like other things,
has been democratised
and if it's true
I have a soul
I'll share it with you.
Not because you are without sin
but mainly because of your pointed, white chin
and in return for your knowing
when I was drowning.
And in return for the nights
when you purred me to sleep
you can keep
your mysterious life.

If it's true –
I have a soul –
I'll share it with you.

Search

The truth we search for
through bewildering worlds
perhaps is somewhere close at hand;
is hidden in a shell,
a blade of grass,
the tiny egg
laid by a willow wren,
a grain of sand.

The shepherds heard the singing.
They were not listening
but half asleep –
tired with the day's round,
resting on the ground.
They were just able
to follow the sheep track down
into the little town
and find the stable.
They did not have to wipe their shoes
or pause to choose
how they would speak.
All was familiar.
The smell of grain and fodder,
animal warmth and slobber.
The new born child asleep.

A star is something very far
up in the sky.
The wise men had to think and know
and plan and plot
before they got

by long and tortuous ways
onto the spot
that they were searching for.
To follow a star
from afar
you need acrobatics
with mathematics.

Far beyond our sky
the secret may lie
within the fourth dimension.
There in the glacial cold
the mystery may unfold.

How do we know
where we should go?
Which are the footprints
in the snow?

Far

How dark it is in outer space.
I shiver with the cold
and I am weightless.
Each familiar thing
which I thought lovely with solidity
is floating round me;
I am floating too.
And in the dark
and cold.

Why did I run away?
How happily I would come home again
to the old world of shapely certainties.
Still the church bells are ringing – but far off,
too far to go. The way is overgrown
and stretches out into infinity,
dizzy with Space and Speed – the Speed of Light.
Light years away the bells are ringing there.

But here on solid earth I am with friends
and I shall go to church with them on Sunday.
The joint is in the oven,
the dog knows it is church day.
He curls up patiently beside the AGA,
where the joint sizzles – there will be a bone.
All this he knows, dreaming in fits and starts
of Sunday afternoon, when somebody
will take him for a walk,
with any luck, through the grey squirrel wood
which leads into the sprawling kitchen garden.
While he dreams, I shall dream

within the family pew, beneath In Memoriam
Tablets, filled with pious sentiments.

How serenely sure
the old world warmly curled around its God,
with earth the centre of the universe.
And yet,
what do we know, how do we know?
We three-dimentional insects, we could not
conceive
of a round world where we could wander
further and further from some given point
in space and find ourselves
back home again, where we had started out.
And if in Space why not in Time?
For both enclose us from infinity
so the way forward may be circular,
the way outward may lead home again.
The tired traveller climbing the last hill
may find, over the ridge, familiar fields.
The same, yet not the same,
the new already seen – the old a fresh vision.
The dog may wake up and his fitful dream
may open into blessed reality
and we may enter that mysterious wood,
where we had dreamt of chasing animals
never, in Time, to be our prisoners
but out of Time, beyond imagined Space
who knows? I know I do not know.

Home
Stray Kitten

Ball of bedraggled fur
encasing a timid alarm clock.
Helpless in a homeless world.

Round the corner of the crumbling street
the hooves of the Four Horsemen
thunder on the asphalt.
Hunger. Fear. Pain. Death by inches in the cold.

Footsteps reverberate in your trembling nerves.
Perhaps it is a boy who will use you for a football.
Perhaps it is a girl who will carry you Home.
Carry you HOME.

Dead[2]

You need not say the word.
I know. I know. I know.
It is not anything
that can be done or undone;
partially mended, possibly remedied,
patched up with shreds of hope,
some chink that lets in light,
some little straw of possible relief.

You need not say the word.
I know the dreaded sound;
like a dull thud – final, irrevocable –
a door which slams
swinging heavily to,
the steel door of a safe.

Nothing will open it,
no key, no tears, no battering human hands,
no fiercest blow lamp
ever made for thieves.
No mighty hammer from Hephaistos' forge;
nothing will move or change
that dreadful thudding word.

You need not say it out.
I see it on your lips.
It hammers at my heart.
I know. I know. I know.

Power Crisis

Fierce, wayward Zeus –
unpredictable as Life –
the Bull of Power,
the Swan of Grace,
had left Olympus in the dark.
No- one had seen him quit the place;
some said
that he was dead.
Juno stopped nagging.
Aphrodite ceased
playing with make-up on her face.
Power left the earth.
The continents began to curl
and wither up like autumn leaves.
The shining eyes of men and beasts
glazed over as in dreadful dearth
and no sound echoed through the mists –
no music from Apollo's lyre,
no shouts from Dionysiac feasts.
The young men ceased to chase away
down country lanes into Pan woods
the giggling nymphs
and at the corners of the streets
stopped wolfish whistling,
stopped dreaming of delicious strife
at close of day.
Like a spent wave
life ebbed away.
And so no wondering men
fell on their knees again
and thanked great Zeus for life.

Then gloomy men with glazing eyes
sat down and wrote lugubrious books.
They were pursued by crabs and doubts
for Zeus had left the bright blue skies.
Some said
that he was dead.
Only the foolish and the freaks
still hoped he might come back again.
Thick clouds obscured Olympic peaks,
the clever ones wrote grimly on;
they analysed – they theorised,
proudly they made a funeral pyre,
a construction,
an abstraction
in sad commemoration
of human liberation.
But finally they ended up,
exhausted by perverse 'affairs'
and sessions of intellectual sex,
devoid of Heaven or hellish thrills –
doubting their own identity.
To cure them of this frightful state
and save them from a zero fate
they were entombed in hospitals
and given electric shocks and pills.
Then suddenly was heard a roar
like distant thunder in the skies;
it came from North and East and West
by fits and starts.
And from the South came sailing swans
with haughty undulating necks;
winged horses rose out of the sea.
No-one saw anything – all was whispered round –

but men and women felt the sap
rising and running through their hearts.
Then on one brilliant starlit night
was heard the sound of pounding hooves.
No- one could say exactly where,
for it was heard on tarmac streets
and strictly forbidden motorways,
in deep and hidden leafy lanes
or thundering past lone farms
on moorland beats.

Radio and television
set up their apparatus.
The County Constabulary
were all alerted.
The Army was called in,
Lord Mayors held conferences,
and citizens made statements;
for modern cities crumbled down
as though some mighty force
had charged –
shattered, the plate glass lay
at break of day
on broken concrete pavements.

No-one reported seeing anything,
except a Puerto Rican
night porter at a smart New York hotel.
He swore
he saw
a bull larger than life with eyes alight
charge bellowing through Manhattan

at dead of night.

Excerpts from **Aphrodite**

(ii)

Tangled in sea-weed,
dizzy with the sun,
warm on my petal flesh
I slid – I rose
into the fragrant, fragile, mortal world.
Sea and sky shimmered
as though washed in gold.
I opened my grey eyes
on the first human I had ever seen.
He was a fisherman.
He had noticed how the dolphins played
about his boat as I lay naked there.
He will die soon not knowing me a goddess –
a goddess tired of gods,
in love with imperfection –
the bitter-sweet of earth.
I told the leaping dolphins
I would stay in their blue world
and love a mortal man;
a part of the growing earth,
the trees, the grass, the running streams, the creatures,
the transient things that grow and live and die
so quietly without complaining.
They are not jealous of the immortal gods,
they come to birth and live and grow and wither
with joy, with fear and understanding nothing.
Beauty and youth they love, yet must they watch
through the long years

time tearing all to shreds.

Anchises is a shepherd on Mount Ida.
He is more beautiful than our immortals;
he herds his cattle in the mountain valleys
where the steep sides are sweet with amaryllis,
anemone and small white clover heads.
He must not know I am a shining goddess
but think me mortal –
a peasant maiden who has lost her way.
I shall ask to meet
his parents and his brothers.
I shall speak dutifully of my parents
and of my dowry.
He will not notice how my doves are cooing
high in those tangled woods.
He will not notice packs of gentle wolves,
gazelles and antelopes all following me,
all happy – all in love with teaming love.
Birds singing to each other, dancing courtship,
hares playing their zigzag games amongst the
boulders.
And when he lays me down upon the flowers,
he will not notice how my body shines –
an opalescent sheen among the grasses –
my breasts like small twin moons
lit by a secret sun.
My little cave concealed
amongst the alluring forest
where lies the hidden secret
of future life.

The herdsman herding cattle in the mountains

must climb and climb
up the steep slopes, across the deep crevasses
where mountain streams break into waterfalls.
Up, winding up to the steep hidden places,
where the clouds float.
I shall come at noon day
when he is drowsing –
there I shall see him,
dozing in the shadow
of wind-tossed trees;
perhaps in tiptoeing
I shall dislodge a pebble
or tread upon a twig.
He will look round.

(iii)

Why did I ever stray from high Olympus
to wander through the earth.
The gates are shut – there is no going back.
Now I know desolation,
the earthly terrors of mortality.
How love is tangled up with death and parting
or worse, with bitterness,
with slow obscene decay.
Death and destruction are my other image.
Ares, you told me this.
I was too young,
I could not understand.
I ran away, but only in a circle.
Here is once more
the smell of blood.
Broken virginity,

the pangs of birth
are all enwoven
like a dreadful tapestry
with blood –
I loved Adonis but he would not love me.

I lay and bared my breasts for him to play with.
He was too shy to look. He ran away,
back to his hunting in the cruel forest.
The wild boar charged – I heard Adonis cry –
and every year I must weep and rejoice.
Weep for the fatal wound – watch life ebbing,
bleeding to death, Adonis soaked in blood –
the sodden earth, anemones turned red,
streams running blood instead of crystal water.
Oh women, weep with me, your lost Adonis.
Wail in my temples, give yourselves to strangers
or if you will not, you must give your hair.
This is what happens if you love a mortal.
The wild boar waits unseen within the wood.
Over the flowering grasses
the dark stream flows.
Yet after the years weeping and heralded by
trumpets
with Dionysiac singing
Adonis will return.
You, Ares, god of battles,
no longer are my lover.
Now we are locked like wrestlers
in mortal conflict.
I match your deathly weapons
with my immortal armour.
My green shoots thrust indomitable

relentless steely blades
through rocks, through mighty walls,
through frozen earth.
I bring
the Spring.

Punic Coin

Triumphant little horse,
proud as Lucifer.
Pricked ears, confident eyes,
arched neck, rippling mane.
And although that is all I see of you,
I am certain your flowing tail
is set high and quivering
with nervous exaltation.
Did you paw with impatience
to move, to race,
to sniff the elixir
of mediterranean sun, sea and air
through those extended nostrils?
What makes you triumphant?
Why do you carry your head
like a Byzantine emperor?
You are much prouder
than most mortals,
yet mortals are told
they are the Sons of God.
They have immortal souls
so why do they not feel triumphant
and walk the earth as you do,
as do the wild animals,
the lions, the leopards,
the antelopes, the gazelles.
Only the animals enslaved to mortals
have lost it;
for they are degraded, tormented
burden carriers, worn out with toil
like most of their masters.

But you – little horses
prance around the Mediterranean
in proud processions,
looking like Sons of God.
Why – why are living creatures
doomed to die?
Are we not all immortal
or all the slaves of death,
maggot ridden obscene decay.
We all love life and long for immortality.

Oh! Power beyond understanding,
give us all your treasured gift.
Make us all Sons of God
or leave us all to worm-ridden disintegration.
Whoever answers – you, my Punic Horse,
you have achieved a sort of immortality.
I shall wear you on my finger
to give me hope.

Ankor Wat

At Ankor Wat
a thousand monkeys play in the trees
above the mysterious city,
abandoned in the jungle,
its massive masonry heeling over
like a ship in a stupendous storm.
Fallen and broken by the implacable power of
growth.

Among the roots and trunks of gigantic trees
the Khmer gods and goddesses lie,
dancing and smiling their secret smile.
Mysterious trinity
of gods and men and surging life.
Above them
a thousand monkeys play in the trees.
Turn – twist – somersault – hoopla,
streak along a branch,
swing by the tail – hoopla – loopla,
chatter to Buddha.
Listen, oh Buddha,
though they do not know it,
their chatter is a prayer
for protection
against snare-cage-aeroplane-vivisection-lab,
all in the name of humanity
who will perhaps benefit.
Oh Buddha,
I would rather take a chance
than imprison these gay snippets of You, of Life
in slavery,

crucifixion,
vivisection.

Oh Buddha,
let them stay,
let them play
in the hot humming air
their brief lives away.

Below them amongst the leaves and lizards
the mighty city crumbles to dust.
There the Khmer gods lie,
still dancing in stone,
still smiling their secret smile
upwards at the sky.

Africa

I am in Africa,
terrible, mysterious, hot-blooded
Africa,
far away from home
but I am not lonely.
I have not moved from my
hidden territory,
my secret family.
I can see in people's eyes
that they recognise me.
The earth is the same.
Things grow in it –
orange and lemon trees,
heavy with fruit.
The oranges fall and lie in the grass,
just as the apples do
in West Country orchards.

I am not lonely.
At night, a beautiful
small grey mini-leopard,
very thin, very elegant,
with great eyes and ears
and pointed chin
like an Egyptian Cat-God
leaps out of the dusky garden
and joins me
with extreme determination.
She curls herself
gracefully into
a grey ring on my bed.

She would like to curl herself round my neck,
but I think this is just a little too intimate
for chance acquaintances.
So she sleeps pressed closely to any part
of my person which protrudes conveniently.
I dare not think of her fate.
She is one of the scrum of hungry cats
who besiege us as we leave the door of the dining-
room.
The others jostle her when they fight for the food
we bring.
Could I dope her and hide her in my luggage?
She is so longing to be loved by some human.

I am not lonely.
By day I exchange secret greetings
with gentle dusky eyes.
The graceful boy who is always on call
is named Mahomet
like everyone else.
He is very friendly
and practises his English on me.
Shaking me by the hand,
when I first arrived,
he said 'Goodbye – How do you – you like it
here?'
As our friendship progressed
and my visit drew to a close,
the thought of tips tarnished slightly,
but not entirely, our relationship.
One day – my friends absent –
he helped me up and down endless steps,
saying 'You are my mother'.

I should have responded
'I am lucky to have such a handsome son'
but could not translate it quickly
into graceful French.

I am not lonely.
The soft slippered peasant woman
dressed in deep glowing coloured skirts
who makes my bed sees the snap
of my husband on the table.
She picks it up.
'Your husband?' 'Yes'
'He is dead?' I nod.
'Ah! C'est la vie'.
A gentle shrug of the shoulders.
'C'est la vie'.

And we are all caught in it together.
That makes it easier to endure.
That is why I see in people's eyes
recognition –
my secret family.

Drumbeat

The sap runs upwards;
the mighty drumbeat of Life
is sounding an alarm.
A green forest- fire sweeps onward,
pale – implacable – arrogant –
the fierce Resurrection of Spring.
The gods are running in the woods,
hair flying, arms and legs entangled
in the wind and the sun.
We also may run,
grasping at their tunics,
kissing what we hold.
In that dark green shadow
I espy a Satyr.
In this flaked sunshine
I glimpse a Nymph – bare.
If you are bold,
if you come quickly,
if you run fleetly,
you may just seize heaven
by the hair.

Mosque

If you can't make Mecca
this will count instead –
so I take a long leap
into the other great faith
which nearly conquered Europe
and I take another leap
back in time.
I gaze through guarded doors
(and past a cloaked figure
with the eyes of a fanatic)
at the marble columns
which Charles Quint swapped
with the Infidels
for the coveted bones of Saints
(or possibly of donkeys and camels.)
I am subdued and uplifted
by this immense polished marble floor,
these wells and fountains of water
(the crystal Sea of Paradise?).
This is great architecture,
comparable to our own cathedrals
and the Byzantine with its entwined arches
I always suspect has some secret in it.
I take another leap – this time in space
and only across the Mediterranean
to our own Byzantine San Marco.
Here are the same mysterious arches,
the gleam of marble and gold
is here on the figures of human Saints,
with Christ triumphant – Christ in agony.

The mosaic floor undulates like the shifting sea's bed,
like poor wavering humanity.
Our radiant Christ was young and impatient,
passionate and compassionate.
He did not write books or evolve a philosophy.
He walked about the hills and shores of Galilee,
healing, smiling at children, comforting outcasts.
Perhaps, Charles, you were deceived by those bones,
but I'm glad you won that battle
somewhere near Vienna
which turned the tide back –
so we still worship our Christ
in our own Byzantine jewel.
Yet somewhere in infinity
some day in eternity
we shall meet together
in that radiancy – so far
only perceived by the mystics
of all the religions –
paradise of our dreams.

News (Vietnam)

After the news at ten o'clock
we'll go to bed.
You must be tired
after that long run in your car.
Turn on the knob
and help yourself to whisky
while we watch:
Police hunting a murderer,
hijackers threatening.
In Ireland pools of blood.
A bleak road. Dying trees.
Army tanks. Refugees.
A small girl struggling along –
her baby brother clinging on
across her hips;
she tries to run –
he is too heavy;
rockets are falling all around.
Behind her rolls the hellish smoke
of village homes burnt to the ground.
She stumbles on distraught with fear.
Why can't I reach that child?
She looks so near.
Turn off the knob –
to left, not right
and let the nightmare world lurch on.
We both looked in on Chris and Clare
so did not hear you come.
Yes, I explained –
they wanted us both there tonight to hear their
prayers

and recitations from school plays –
as well as all three teddy bears.

Did we remember to switch on
our electric blanket?
Switch off the heat
on the first floor?
Have we put out the cat?
Bolted the kitchen door?
Otherwise all the world's spilt blood
might seep in across the mat.
Do you like a bath?
The water is always hot.
Breakfast is nine-ish.
Do you like an egg?
And tea or coffee?
The bath and loo is on your right
across the passage.
Could you switch off the light?
Tomorrow if it's fine at all
we'll take the car
and picnic by the waterfall.
Gentle Jesus meek and mild
what happened to that child?
Yes – on your right.
Good night.
Sleep well.
Oh! Hell.

Beware

Oh careful housewife,
beware, beware!
Where the wild creatures of the jungle crouch –
pitiless Aphrodite,
terrifying Pan,
Zeus who hurls his indiscriminate thunderbolts,
blue veined Poseidon who can whirl
calm seas into tumult.
They lurk behind the linen chest
where lie the spare pillows and blankets
encased in cellophane;
in the cupboard where the cups and glasses
are ranged upside down
to keep out the dust.
In the fly-proof larder,
under the mouse-proof bin.
Beware, beware!
Be careful for your children
who need the cliff of security
and the hedge of love
to shelter them from the cold of this world
and the consuming fires of Hell.
The attested milk may be in the refrigerator,
the First Aid box may be full –
tubes for burns and bruises,
bandages for all parts of the body,
disinfectants for infections,
anti-tetanus, anti-biotic,
Aspirin – Anadin-
tranquiliser – pep pill.
But nothing from Heaven or Hell

to tame the unruly heart.

So, careful housewife,
loyal mate, devoted mother,
sweep out the neglected box- room,
look under the fitted carpet,
where the wild creatures of your jungle lurk.
Beware!

Superior People

How sad Superior People are
and how they mope and wail.
They read the dismal daily news
within the Daily Telegraph
or worse, the Daily Mail.
They moralise, they warn and sigh.
They never guess what's brewing.
New hopes – new movements – new ideas –
new prospects pass them by.
They all vote Tory to a man
and to a grumbling woman
complaining that her Daily
makes her cleaning bills enormous
and her Jobbing Gardener's wages
are ridiculously high.
Superior People seldom laugh.
They criticise and sigh.

How sad Superior People are.
They only know a few
Superior People like themselves
who talk and think and act
as Superior People do.

They never really mix with those
they think of lower station.
Such people they consider lack
Good Taste and Education.
Their voices jar, they have no mind
and so Superior People miss
the taste – the splendid brew –

the infinite variety
of jostling human kind.

Geriatric Ward
An old man

Tomorrow at 8.30, zero hour,
we start the Revolution at the docks.
Why have you put me in this bloody hole.
Don't interrupt – it's you that makes me swear.
There is so much to do. Christ! Must I tell you
you are wasting time – we must get going now.
The world is full of dirt and wickedness.
If we could get rid of Capitalists
everything would come right – don't interrupt me.
Every man should have the right to work.
That's basic – that is why I joined the Party.
The Party stood for that.
We got to bash the Tories and the Bosses.
We got to work and work together too
not like a lot of snarling animals
but like the brothers that we know we are.

Don't shut me up then – what the bloody hell
is wrong with what I'm saying?
You know it's true, it echoes in your hearts.
I'm shouting so that all the ward can hear.
Well, don't you shout then – come and listen to
us.
We hold our meetings at the Institute
and sometimes at the dock gates – in the street.
I'm secretary of the District Branch.
Every man should have the bloody right
to work and treat his mates like pals and brothers.
My Dad he was a Durham miner's son.
He made me fight and know what I was at.

So did my Mam. She was an Irish girl
from County Mayo.
So did my Nancy with the shock of hair
and eyes as green as emeralds.
She's old now – crippled up with artheritis.
She can't well lift the kettle off the hob
without I'm there to help her.
So I must get along,
I can't stop here.

Tomorrow at 8.30 they'll be there.
Well, what I mean it's urgent, absolutely.
In Cannon Street - that lies along the river
by the gasometers.
(It's down now, all excepting old Ma Brown
at the corner shop, they couldn't get her out.
She wouldn't budge when all them coppers come
she threw her chamber pot at Boss's head).

In Cannon Street we lived at Number Ten
and all the folks there called me Fighting Tim.
All right, who'll fight me then? I'll take 'em on.
Well, what I mean, men are thrown out of work,
the kids'll suffer.
We must fight the Bosses.
All the street turned out – men and women – kids.
Building a barricade against the coppers.
Some bloke spoke fine – we marched alone with
placards.
Banners and slogans – old arm chairs and
bedsteads.
I can't remember what it was about.
Don't interrupt me – I am at work – on duty.

I'm picketing. We've blacked that bloody cargo.
If they bring in non-union men, we'll bash'em
tomorrow morning all me pals and me.
We meet at 8 o'clock where the dock wall
is scrawled all up with slogans.
Slogans about – I can't rightly remember.
Don't waste my time. Take all this shit away.
Where are me clothes. Some bastard must 'a
pinched 'em.
Well, what I mean, where am I?
I'm wasting time. This place is bloody Hell –
Mary, Queen of Heaven,
it's Fighting Tim, baptised a Catholic.
Pray for us all and get us out of here.
This place is bloody Hell.
All right, all right – I'm praying
not swearing – don't you shout at me.
To hell with all that mucky stuff in glasses.

Don't give me pills – a kid with bellyache
is what you take me for – I'm Fighting Tim.
And don't you try to boss me.

There's only one here that can give me orders
and she's the Sister, bosses all the Ward.
That's not the reason. It's her eyes that gets you.
Full lidded eyes that shine like stars in heaven
and make a bloke like me go into dreams
of Queens and Saints and Heavenly Hostesses.
She's off this evening. Take that shit away.
Where are my clothes? Same bloody chap has
pinched 'em.
I am not shouting. I'm informing you.

The meeting is tonight – it's down at Bill's.
The Institute is booked – we couldn't get it.
I'm secr'try and I must open up.
And don't you try to stop me.
If you lock me in,
I'll smash my way out through the window panes
or knock the bloody place down.
Mary, Queen of Heaven,
come down from Paradise.
Come with your heavy lidded eyes,
so full of light and mercy
and green as emeralds.
Rescue us all and get us out of here.
And lead us – lead us shouting.
All right – all right it isn't only me.
It's the whole world.

Geriatric Ward
An old woman

The door is locked. Here in this stranger place
life seems to end and only dreams go on.
I only dream that I am going home.
To home and all the old familiar places.
I find the back door with the water butt
and the milk cans that stand upon the cobbles.
We never use the front door for ourselves.
The back door nearly always stands ajar.
It's shabby now. The paint is peeling off
where Boxer used to scratch to be let in.
Always liked company – the sound of voices.
He's buried over yon close by the rickyard
still within sound of footsteps and the like.
Which is the way home? Down the long corridor?
Painted bright yellow to make us think
we've got outside into the summer sun.
No. That leads only to the lavatory –
only the lavatory door stands always open.
I am so old. I often lose my way.
And people lead me back. They call me 'Love'.
But do not love me, only pity me.
I must be getting home. In this hot weather
the milk turns sour – should be kept in the porch.
The cool flagged porch – there is no other way.
Janet and Tom said I should have a fridge
but even in summer I never wasted nowt.
Such new contraptions wouldn't work for me.
Any time now the pullets start to lay.
I know where they will go.
No-one else finds the eggs

unless I get them now, they will be lost.

I must go home tomorrow.
The door is locked. They always hide the key.
Some folks can find it. Someone showed me once
but I am old – I have forgotten where -
and people lead me back.
Past the great kitchen full of steel and steam,
past the grand room where doctors come and go.
Only the lavatory door stands always open
for folk like me who often lose their way.
And old men fumbling at their genitals.
For some have lost their way
and some have lost their memories
of where and who they are.
So the front door is locked to keep us in.
There is one way to get outside they say.
A hard and bitter way. I have not found it.
Janet and Tom won't tell me, when they come to
see me.
They turn aside my talk
with bits of news of home
and sometimes a few flowers, a pot of jam.
The garden isn't tended
since I came here.
No-one has time for it
but there are still some roses
growing among the thistles and the docks
although no-one has pruned or fettled them.
And little Tom, he went and gathered some
and brought them here for me.
They did not last long in this hot, dry air.
Not very often – every now and then.

My other lads come bringing me their news
of homes and children. Robert has left school
and been apprenticed to a carpenter.
Carole is courting.
Jessica has been
to get her tonsils out in hospital.
(There they don't lock the door).
Dick, the scholar,
has passed some things called O's and A's at
school.

Through the high windows of the common room
I can look out and see a field of barley
and it is turning, with this sunny weather.
The glass is set, September dews upon us.
The harvest will begin; then I must go.
'Not yet', they say, 'not yet – just wait a bit
till you are stronger.'
'I can't wait any longer, they will need me.
The girl and Janet can't do all the baking
without me there to help – the harvest teas,
they take a lot of extra fettling on.'
The barley field is turning.
I must go home, I must go home tomorrow.
Where are my shoes?
I can't go out in slippers.
Someone has tidied them – not in the locker
nor under the high bed –
I must go home, I must go home tomorrow.
The harvest –

Country Wedding

The church is full.
Matrons erect, irate.
The guardians of home
rules and moralities
draped in faked fur
with flowering hats
topping their features
set as hard as marble.
Beside them sit
their sweating mates
dressed in dark serge,
too tight for mortal comfort.
Among the hassocks many children scramble,
partially anchored
by parental guards -
families of Bride and Groom,
they flank the aisle down which
the pair will come like captives,
hemmed in and driven to market.

There is a stir.
The Bride arrives,
dressed up, but still deliciously
in disarray;
pulled, pinched and prodded
into tight white satin,
shining and straining on her ripening body
her swelling breasts and womb.
She wears a modish head -dress,
but her thick hair
has pushed it out of trim.

It was not meant to be confined by fashion
but to be spread upon the flowering grasses
or mixed with beech mast,
the same tawny colour.
The congregation stiffens:
'Quite four months gone'
is passed from mouth to mouth.
'Or perhaps five'.
The fruit of summer courting
down by the rick yard,
out upon the meadows
of drying grass, smelling of clover heads
or in some hollow
by a hedgerow tree.

It is high noon,
nothing is stirring.
The small birds
sleep in the shallow runnels
of the corn,
or the deep shadows
of great turnip loaves.
The cows are lying down
and so is she.
Frightened, he looks upon
her naked loveliness,
the sacrificial victim
laid out upon the flowery altar, earth.
She waits in fear and rapture -
the final, fatal thrust.
Her blood will stain the grasses.
The wood anemones' innocent white
will turn red once again

as when Adonis lay
and bled to death
in Aphrodite's arms.
The buttercups and daisies
will bend in the heavy dew
of Aphrodite's tears.

Over the hedgerow
in the silent wood
among the curled dead leaves
of oak and sycamore
there is the faintest rustling tread.
It sounds like cloven hooves
but there are no cloven- footed beasts
in Farthings Breach.
Among the twigs and the light printed footmarks
lies a grey feather
from a pigeon's breast
and there are always pigeons
in Farthings Breach.
But this is strangely bright.
It shines like silver
in the bosky gloom.
Could it have been a dove?
A dove flown out from Paphos,
blown off its course by summer winds
and into Farthings Breach?

Spring Salute

The stone is rolled away.
The sky is full of singing.
On earth the sap is rising,
Arjuna draws his sword,
Druids salute the sun,
Osiris kisses Isis,
Adonis moves again
'mongst his anemones
dyed red with blood.
The Christ, the Christ is risen.
You will not recognise Him in the Garden.

Compassion

Compassion is not a gentle thing.
It is a fierce intolerable scourge,
a fever in the blood without a cure,
a slave tormenter with a knotted whip
driving you into slums and hospitals,
ghettos where drug addicts lie sprawled around.
Camps for refugees
where you may die, in filth, of cholera
or slowly, week by week, of malnutrition.

Vainly imploring in Gethsemane
through Golgotha and on to Calvary
you stagger with the heavy draining Cross
compassion puts on your aching back.
Only at Calvary you lay it down
and then it takes you up
to die in agony, without the myrrh,
without the vinegar.
'My God why hast thou thus forsaken me?'
The soldiers laugh.

Sunday Morning

Small congregation,
getting smaller. Dull sermon.
Who was that man
sitting with Miss Furbelow?
Wind up the clocks.
Yet time is running out.
Let out Jemima
lest she pee on the hall carpet.
Take her for a turn.
But there's nowhere now to go.
There are no horses left
in the Georgian stables,
there are no carrots left
and no kitchen garden.
It didn't pay, we let it
to a vulgar market gardener.
Now it grows cabbage
for the local supermarket.
Over the horizon
children with great bellies
and wide imploring eyes
are shrivelling up from hunger.
Have a glass of sherry
to forget that dull sermon.
The joint is sizzling hot,
punctual as usual.
So wind up the clocks.
Yet time is running out.

Teresa's Song

Land's End. Land's End.
No more dustbins. No more cops.
No more pavements. No more lorries.
No more adverts. No more shops.

All the dirt washed off in water,
rolling waves and swirling rings.
In the shining sea are fishes,
in the shining air are wings.

Coombe

Now the whole earth is growing,
calmly and silently, inexorably.
The great sun swings across the dome of sky,
the shadows shorten, wheel and lengthen out,
tied to his flame which no power can delay.
The green sap rises, the green world unfurls,
the eternal miracle returns again.
Here there is quietness and time to watch
the insect climbing up the blade of grass
with its transparent shadow –
both moving like two dancers in the breeze.
The shadows lengthen – evening's yellow light
drenches the meadows, woods and cottages.
For an enchanted hour all turns to gold.
Then comes the night; but stealthily and quietly
the growth goes on although the sun has gone.
The solid earth we knew has vanished quite
and in its place a phantom world appears,
an apparition in a silver trance;
so bright, yet so entirely insubstantial.
The only solids, shadows black as pitch.
The moon is full.
Mysterious phantom light
flakes in between the crevices of curtain
upon my bed.
Shall I awake tomorrow
a shadowy lunatic?
No, a new sun will appear in time
like a young king, all power and arrogance.
Earth will be born again in innocence
and every bud will glitter in the light.

The sky will turn blue
for it needs to frame
the white blossom of the early plum.
Tomorrow is Good Friday –
tomorrow all good folks will go to church
and afterwards put in their seed potatoes.
They cannot fill the church with daffodils
in readiness for Easter until three,
when Christ hangs dead upon the cruel cross;
so life and death contend as they have done
through immemorial time – and out beyond it.
The sun wheels, the universe revolves;
the resurrection happened in a garden
where Mary thought she saw the gardener
but looked again and knew it was her Love.

(Maundy Thursday 1978)

Whitsun

The church is full of flowers.
It must be Whitsuntide.
White lilac, crimson peonies.
The altar hangings
are red and gold.

This is the Festival of Flames,
of Tongues and Inspiration,
of Magic Words
which pierce like swords and spears
the human heart.

To celebrate
we hear Isaiah's golden worded dream
of Peace and Love.
The Lion and the Ox, the Little Child.
We hear a poet's royal psalm of life.
Finally we hear Paul's trumpet blast,
challenging Principalities and Powers
and creatures –
the whirling galaxies light years away,
matter dissolving into energies.
The chemical reactions of the brain.
The terrifying empty glacial spaces
which cannot freeze our hearts
or separate us from the love of God.

Dazed with the power of words we totter out
into the flaming green of early June.
How can we go straight home and cook the
supper –

we must move on and find the Holy Mountain,
join with Isaiah's innocent procession –
the leopard and the kid, the cow, the bear,
the timid calf, the cockatrice and asp.
And gambling in from David's Psalm of Life
the wild goats come – the coneys leave their
rocks.
Peonies of crimson crown the Lion's head,
white lilac wreaths the Ox's twisted horns.
The child will lead us with his daisy chain;
He knows the pathway to the Holy Mountain.

June

A green tidal wave
submerges the Earth.
It has flooded everything;
it has conquered us all.
Grasses, weeds, flowers,
blossoming trees
thrust their indomitable way
up to the light.
And in the night
immense, peach coloured – a balloon
rises behind the ink-black trees
into the dark blue sky
of June.
It must be
the moon.

Under the flowering chestnut trees
prowling through wild parsley jungle
a black tiger cat
wails for a mate
to the moon,
to the sky.
He would like
to people the Earth
with black tiger cats,
elegant as himself -
with curling white whiskers
and green reproachful eyes.
Why?
I wonder why?

I wonder why
the irresistible force of life
thrusts upwards
towards the sky,
uncurling, sprawling, spreading.
I join the black cat.
I wail to the moon,
to the sky,
to the stars,
to Venus and Mars
for a mate
throughout June.
But WHY?
Tell me, WHY?

Christmas

The light grew dark, the sun shone dim.
The earth slept, dreaming of the spring.
A shiver ran through Mammon's fat,
a girl's voice sang 'Magnificat'.

Christmas Dialogue

She:
Hang up the mistletoe,
light up the candles on the Christmas tree.
Where did we hide the presents for the children?

He:
This is no Christian Festival of Love.
We celebrate the Roman Saturnalia.
The Lord of Misrule
staggers through Bethlehem.
Old Saturn reigns again.
There was no miracle,
no shepherds and no singing,
no dreaming Joseph,
no wise men following a star.
There is no mention in the Early Gospel.
All that was added later, scholars say.

She:
It was the shepherds first who heard the singing
and saw the star and found the cattle shed.
The wise men with their learned calculations
took longer to arrive.

He:
There was no miracle.

She: All births are miracles.
All wombs are sacred vessels carrying life.
Mary was in love
with God or Gabriel or some shining Boy.

Mankind is always dreaming of a God –
hang up the mistletoe.

He:
And join the Druids worshipping the sun?
Their symbol is erotic –
why do we kiss beneath the mistletoe?

She:
Because we worship life –
adored fertility
and we must conquer death.
So we must have
the Rising in the Spring –
the Shining Ones
forever love and die and rise again.
Osiris torn to pieces,
Adonis gored by the boar,
bleeding to death
in Aphrodite's arms.
And now our Christ,
born while the angels sang,
dying in agony
and winning back to life –
the empty tomb.

He: Osiris' tomb.

She: And Christ's.
So we continue
worshipping always
love and fertility,
always the mother

with her first-born child.
After the joy, the agony of loss.
Isis searching the rice fields,
Demeter calling out
for lost Persephone
and grey-eyed Aphrodite,
wet with Adonis' blood,
Mary, the Mother,
Magdalene, the Lover,
all, all the women whose shining ones
were torn from their arms
and mangled on battlefields –
all crouch by the dreadful cross
and weep their hearts out,
while the soldiers laugh
and cast their lots
and play their games of chance.
They know they cannot guard
the empty tomb.

Hang up the mistletoe
and let us kiss,
before we light the candles on the tree –
where did we hide the presents for the children?

Songs for Magnificat
Open the Door

Open the door.
It's warm inside,
there's a glittering chandelier.
It's light inside.
There's dancing on the floor.
Open – open the door.
Inside there's a band,
very grand,
dressed up in red and gold.
If you're cold,
red looks good.
On the floor
a red carpet
and shiny wood
where they dance
and prance.
On the tables there's food.
It smells good.
There's shiny glasses
full of wine
and waiters in red and gold.
In this gaddam Hell
everything is bought and sold
but we've nothing to sell.
There's no jobs around here,
so we can't buy.
Hi!
Mister!
Open the door.
Please, mister, bring us wine

and chicken on a shiny dish,
all covered in sauce,
to make us dance
and prance
on the floor.

Mister – if you go to church,
there they tell you sure
to help the poor.
So – Mister – open –
open the door!
What's more, if you don't
we'll smash it in.
Would that be sin?
Yes – in a capitalist world
but not in ours, you swine,
so bring us food and wine.
When wolves are hungry,
they attack
and in a pack –
so stand back.
The carpet is red,
so it won't show
blood –
blood will mix with wine
fine.
If the chicken is finished,
give us bread –
bread and wine.
That boy who was murdered
had a last meal with his pals,
and gave them bread and wine.
He knew about hunger.

He guessed about death.
He said
the wine was his blood –
both red.
Wine they still drink.
It's his blood they still think.
But it's turned into a play –
symbolic
they say.
They aren't hungry no more.
They aren't poor.
So stop play -acting
and open – open – open the door.

Herod Augustus

No, Your Highness, they aren't coming back;
never coming back this way
they say.
They aren't calling in as they said they would.
Someone had a dream.
They thought Your Highness could
kill the baby king.
So
no-one would know.

Herod Augustus – rest assured
he won't come back.
He's gone abroad,
they say.
Over the border a long, long way
into Egypt – the mythical land.
Towards mirage – across the sand,
over the mountains no man has crossed –
across the rivers no man can ford.
Herod Augustus. He's gone abroad.

Yes, Your Highness. He will come back.
Get ready the torturer's nails and rack;
keep in with the folks who wield the power.
Arm the police, call up the forces.
Give suspect personnel the sack.
Use any means – use all resources.
Herod Augustus – he will come back.

First Footing

New Year's Eve,
midnight.
On the church clock
midnight has struck.
Will a Dark Man come
First Footing
to bring me luck?

It's cold outside.
In the frozen black
white snowflakes
whirl round the icy track
which leads to the east door
of my Georgian shack.

Midnight has struck.
Will a Dark Man come
to bring me luck?
With the copper coin,
with the lump of coal,
with the slice of bread
to keep together
my body and soul.

Footsteps on the frozen snow.
The bell rings.
He is here.
Open the door.
Clothcap, muffler, greatcoat
flecked over with snow.
Come in, come in!

I know you – I know
your dark eyes,
shining so bright
in the light
from the passage.
So very bright –
are there tears in them?
Come in, come in
to the light.
Yes – tears.
I was right.

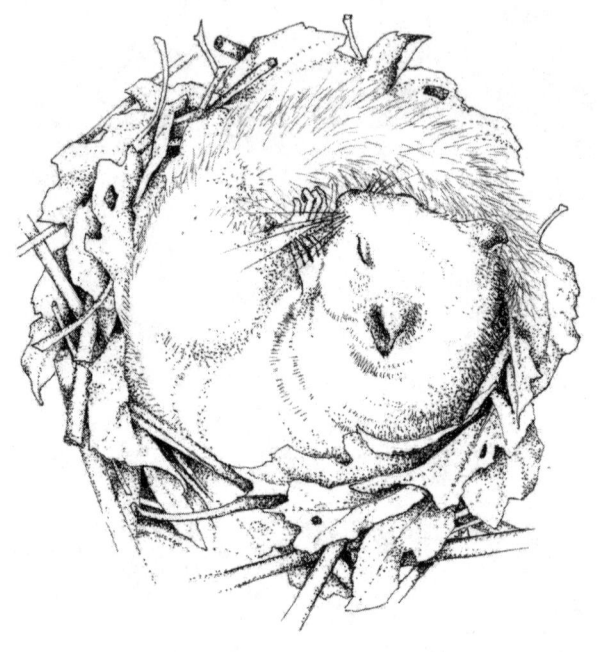

Doggerel for Winter

The rabbit and the stoat
have grown their winter coat.
Deeply in the earth
the snail has burrowed down.
The dormouse is in bed,
his tail over his head
-a tiny russet ball,
the smallest mouse of all.
Within the thickest gorse bush
he can find
which keeps out snow and wind.

The mackerel streaks away
to find a warmer strand.
The chiff-chaff and the willow wren
fly to a sunnier land.
The cuckoos and the warblers
have flown away to Africa.
The swifts have taken flight,
the swallows follow after.
The moth and butterfly,
immobilised and beautiful,
in odd house crannies lie.

I am foolish – I am old.
Keep me warm,
out of storm.
I am helpless – I am old.
Keep my heart from growing cold.

November 24th

Now the dusk deepens,
earth crumbles into twilight.
November's silver sun – turned dying red –
has sunk behind the wood's
black tracery of trees.
Clouds drift across the sky –
flocks of grey sheep
driven before the wild, wild wind,
the west wind of November.
This is the dreaming twilight
before the winter Solstice.

Outside my window
a dark bird perches
on the bare branches
of the yellow rose.
Swaying in the windy dusk
as I sway slung between
my Past and Future.
Within a week
I shall be born.
Already I am stirring
within my mother's womb,
soon I shall start the struggle
into the world,
wrapped in the womb of Time.

A bird
flying in from the dark
through the lighted room
and out again into darkness.

Darkness or Light?

Nightmare

Keep out of my dreams.
Keep off – keep out.
No, I did not dream about you,
of course not. Quite the contrary.
Actually, I dreamt about a bear
who wanted me to play with him.
But I knew what that meant,
that terrifying hug,
crushing me to death –
my thoughts, myself, my soul,
oozing away in black annihilation.
Just a nightmare really –
a bear
in its lair.

Keep out of my dreams.
Keep off. Keep out.
Of course it wasn't you –
just a nightmare;
because I ate
much too late
toasted cheese.
And because I am a fool
I forgot to keep my rule
not to eat it late at night.
And this was much, much, much
too late.

Then a serpent came
and threatened me.
Perhaps I had been reading

Genesis
much, much, much
too late.

It reared up over me;
its blood-shot eyes
stared through my body –
it was about to make
the fatal thrust.

No, I did not. No, I did not,
I did not dream of you –
of course it wasn't you,
just a nightmare.
You see, I have discovered
that once a person penetrates
one's dream,
steps over the boundary
into the deep stream –
the subterranean river
that flows beneath the Earth –
there may be trouble brewing.
The poison may have entered
the blood stream.
So –
it may be
much, much, much
too late
to call a doctor in.
No.
I did not dream of you.
There's no way into me
through dreams –

it seems.

After these nightmares – as I woke –
alone and cold and all forlorn,
I saw a milk-white unicorn,
erect, against a blood red dawn.

Lament

Who am I waiting for?
My lovers are all dead.
And if I call, they cannot come to me
if I wake crying in the fearful night.
No-one will comfort me.

What am I waiting for?
The final kiss
which strips from the grinning skull
the velvet skin
and dims the shining living eyes of love,
closing the lips forever?

Why am I listening for the sounds
I shall not hear again?
Familiar footsteps – voices in the dark –
the secret revelations between lovers.
I shall lie down upon the ground
but I shall stay there.
Someone will close my eyes, but open them no more.
I shall not see the flowering grasses
and the great sky above me.
I shall not feel my lover's weight –
only the weight of earth –
nor shall I rise and stare about a world
newly created by an ancient god.

I shall not see again
a man's face drained of blood and ashy white
because I walked into a crowded room.

I was so young then, I did not know
how Aphrodite reigns
over the ebb and flow of human hearts
as the moon does the everlasting sea,
swinging the implacable tides which lap our earth.

I shall not hear again
the breathless words
that make or unmake lives.
I shall only hear
the doors creaking in the empty house,
the dust settling,
the sound of scratching, scuffling mice
which rhymes with small talk – silly gossiping
friends –
aimless activities to fill in time.
So why do I linger?
Why?

Widow

Why are they taking you away
out into the cold hard ground?
The sky is grey – it looks like rain,
you will be lonely, you will be desolate.
I am waiting for you here by the fire.
Your chair is still there, opposite mine.
I am waiting for you to come home.
The light is fading, it looks like rain.
But of course – I forgot -
we want rain.
Those seeds we sowed together
will never come through in the border
without rain.
The earth is hard as concrete –
too hard to lie on.
You need something soft for your head.
My breasts are still soft,
though they will never be filled with milk again
for our children.
Our children are grown men and women –
the miracle we conjured together.
But the earth is hard as concrete,
no seed could germinate in it.
What was it someone said about seeds?
They die, but in dying
something more is born – and grows.
The grain of wheat, the sheaf of corn.
So when we die –
could it be true, if I wait long enough?
No, I want you now,
I want you here.

I want your footsteps outside
and the door to open.
I want to feel your body in my arms
and then, like a watered plant,
come to life,
laugh and exchange news,
put the kettle on for tea.
Where have you gone,
why don't you come home?
It's late – very late.
You were never as late as this.
The light is fading – it looks like rain.
It's cold – it's getting dark.
You must be tired.
Come home, come home
and lay your head between my breasts.
Oh love! Where are you now?
Come home.

The Intruder (2)

Don't go – Don't go.
Oh! Please don't leave me so.
Yes, yes, I know,
I told them I was not at home
to you.
To keep you out,
send you away,
say
you were a tramp – a stranger,
INTRUDING,
whom I did not know
so
you would not interrupt my life.
Please go
or if you stay
don't drag me – hustle me
away
into your world.
How can I live in two?

Don't touch,
don't kiss;
for if you do
remembered bliss
will come again.
I shall remember
what I miss.

Please go – please go,
before this smouldering world
catching a spark

from your enchanted torch
bursts into flame.
Don't go – don't go
Oh! Please don't leave me
so
blindfold and lame.

House

The house is empty now,
the paint is flaking,
on the west door long streaks of naked wood
show where a dog once scratched to be let in.
The kitchen has some shabby patches too,
the corner of the dresser is rubbed bare
by an impatient cat awaiting food.
When the wind whistles round the house and
garden,
a passer-by might hear the children's voices
in the long nursery passage where the plaster
is peeling off under the window frames.
In the summerhouse there is a gate-legged table.
The top has crumbled into dust but over it
some rotting matting makes it into a cave –
a lair – a tent – a perfect children's 'house',
a children's house where mother made a 'Home',
dispensing birthday treats and tea parties
to younger members of the family.
About it there still lie
remains of feastings. Doll-size cups and saucers,
miniature plates which once held birthday cakes
made of rose leaves, flower petals, daisy heads
and tiny fir -cones hidden in the grass.
The inmost corners of the summerhouse
are heaped with leaves, blown in from many
autumns
and here a hedgehog makes her nest
and hides her young.
Outside the summerhouse in the low wall
which skirts a mossy terrace

there is a tiny door
leading in old days to a water tap.
The children thought it was a fairies' house
but if it was they shared it with a field mouse.
One summer day, I saw her coming out,
leading a family tail of baby mice –
exquisite reproductions of herself
but miniscule, so small, so perfect were they –
miracles of creation by a mother.

No sound disturbs the summer- house today.
No-one breaks in to fetch the cricket stumps,
no high pitched voices quarrel over games,
no birthday parties sitting on the grass
pretend to eat and drink and smoke cigars.

But when the west wind lashes round the garden
perhaps the far off sound of children's voices
is heard, so faint that they might even be
fairies or field mice.
Yet if you called and peered into the laurels –
those magic laurels, full of children's dreaming,
untended, overgrown, with hollow caverns
perfect for pirates, robbers and Indians –
no-one would answer you.

Goodwill towards Men

Hullo! Hullo!
Brown brother,
black sister.
Good morning. Good day.
Look out! Look out!
Wicked men may
blow up our world.
But say
we like it this way –
we like the blue sky,
the black velvet night,
the twin balls up aloft
of silver and gold
look all right.
We like
our brown living Earth
with its green flame of growth,
not a red flame of death.
Oh! Stop those bad men
who may burn up our Earth.
Our boys and our girls
want to live. Not to die.
They love the brown Earth,
they love the blue sky.
They want to be happy
to work and to play,
to dance in the sunshine.
To stay
if they
may.

[1] Ruth was inspired to write this poem when she had invited her relative James Hugonin to stay at Ormesby Hall and enabled him to use the kitchen in the Old Hall as his artist's studio. His friend Sarah (now his wife) joined him after a while and it was the loving relationship between them that moved Ruth. They were both at the beginning of their careers as artists and they enjoyed the freedom, space and ambience which Ruth and Ormesby Hall were able to offer.

[2] This poem was a reaction to the sudden death of Ruth's friend Kathleen Cooper Abbs who lived at Mount Grace Priory. She tragically died at the age of 73 in 1974 whilst attempting to swim around the pier at Saltburn in order to raise money for two local churches, those of East Harlsey and Ingleby Arncliffe, North Yorkshire.